THE DOVES C

For Lesley
with love,

Julia

JULIA CASTERTON

THE DOVES
OF FINISTERRE

A *The Rialto*
First Edition

ACKNOWLEDGEMENTS

Acknowledgements are due to the editors of the following maga-
zines, who first published some of these poems: *Ambit*, *Heat*
(Australia), *Magma*, *The London Magazine*, *The North*, *The Rialto*, *Staple*.

One poem appeared in the catalogue of Lino Mannocchi's
Annunciation exhibition, one in a Forward Collection, one in Poems
for Mordechai Vanunu (Campaign to free Vanunu), one in a *Staple*
anthology, one in the *Parents* anthology (Enitharmon), two in *In The
Company of Poets* (Hearing Eye), several in *Sestet* (Staple) and some in
As Girls Could Boast (The Oscars Press).

First published in 2004 by
The Rialto
PO Box 309 Aylsham Norwich
England NR11 6LN

ISBN 09527444-6-5
The publisher acknowledges financial assistance from the Arts
Council of England, East.

The Rialto is a Registered Charity No. 297553
Typeset in Perpetua 10 on 12.5pt
Design by Starfish, Norwich www.starfishlimited.com
Printed by Printing Services (Norwich) Limited

For CJN, mvp.

CONTENTS

HERE IS THE ROOM

Here is the room. It shines. It breathes its scent of night flowers
So as not to intrude on thought, or sleep, or conversation
With oneself. Much light, but filtered, perhaps through marble
Cut to inch-thin amber stillness. When dark's needed,
One can draw screens of stained glass, glass the colour of
Icelandic ice-floes, Galician green, or the slow mauve
Of autumn sunlight just before horizons slip away.

If words are longed for, all words, spoken or unspoken,
Are walking down the mind's wide corridors,
Informally, as friends who come and go
But don't live here. The host is silence, who's arranged the room
With such slow sweetness, there is really nothing more to say.

One lives here. Not I or you, but one for whom
Personality, attributes, and all desire and pain
Have somehow dropped and fallen away, and disappeared,
Or become the scent of night flowers.

VIGIL

'What you've never had you've never missed,' my
mother told the curate with one hand
who sat with us the week my sister died.

He wore a leather glove over his shy
left hand. The neighbours visiting looked stunned.
'What you've never had you've never missed,' my

mother laughed, his missing hand the only
moment of relief when we were dumbfound.
We hardly spoke the week my sister died.

'You could be right,' good-humoured, he replied,
and looked down gently at his good right hand.
What you've never had you've never missed. My

mother knew her blunder straightaway. Her smile
faded. Some part of her, unsafe, but sound,
that sat with us the week my sister died

never thought much of her own slow suicide,
rejection of three daughters still to hand.
'What you've never had you've never missed,' my
mother said. We missed her from the week my sister died.

WAITING

At some time perhaps it always comes to this,
that you sit by a narrow hospital bed
and wait
as others in the room are waiting by other beds
for someone to tip towards living or dying.

Perhaps you weigh up your time with this someone,
weighing how much you've hated them and how much loved.
You count the wasted time and the drenched with fullness time
and wait.
And the face in the bed and the body you take care of in the bed

compose themselves, while you are waiting, into
tired, pursued love. Love at the end of its rope.
And you are part of the love they have become,
part of the bedpan-carrying, soiled sheets school of love,
as are the others in the room, waiting

for others still to tip towards living or dying.
The others mirror your own fatigue
in the battle of tired love
where you let yourself go
and fatigue takes love beyond itself.

And all the people in the room
including those whose tipping towards life or death
is being waited for,
are astonished at what they have become
when they thought they were only waiting.

RESOURCES

For sleeping between two chairs at the hospital -
two books, which I place under my head,
and a cotton shawl from India, maroon and cream batik,
to lay across my legs.

Of the books, one is Chekhov's stories in Spanish,
which I don't read,
and one a life of Lorca,
which I do.

In his last days
hiding out in the house of a fascist friend,
and in his last hours
in the holding house far from anywhere

before they gave him *lots of coffee*,
the code for *shoot him*,
I am there in the olive grove
with the old teacher chained to him

and he is here with me
perhaps wrapped in my Indian shawl,
the knowledge of his last hours in my vigil by your bed,
the knowledge of my vigil by your bed in his last hours.

'BIRDS BUILD, BUT NOT I BUILD'

Gerard Manley Hopkins.

And where the Galicians haven't built, around this hospital,
The buddleia's crowded in to make its own houses
As it does on London's waste ground.

But here, it's entered into a pact with purple morning glory,
Marigolds, Russian vine, wild roses, in a ravel of living.
A living house. Though there's nowhere to rest in the hospital,
Here I could lie down.

'WE SHOULD HAVE PUT YOUR ENGLISH ON MORPHINE LONG AGO'

Sabbath's Theatre, Philip Roth.

When I return from my little meal, you have it in your mind
That I come bearing *chuletas de ternera*.
'So! You've got a stove in the toilet,' you say cunningly.
'That was good thinking.'

I follow your mind through its maze of morphine
Loving the connections I'd never made before.
Why not a stove in the toilet, after all?
With a foldaway bed it could be the word's smallest flat.

Galicia colludes in the magic of the drug.
When I cross the dual carriageway, I find on spare land underneath
A woman and a man smelling remarkably like goats
With their flock munching on briars, marigolds, cardboard.

They herd them up the steps and down the pavement of the carriageway
While I cross the bridge back to you, bearing El Mundo
So you can choose a film. The air fills with vanilla and honey
From the *habitacion* of buddleias festooned with Russian vine.

Que dia, my love. A day to be alive in.

BLOOD WEDDING

Now you can walk to the toilet
As the urgency inside increases
But, stumbling, you forget the two bottles of blood
Draining through tubes from the wound in your belly
And they rattle along the floor of the ward
So I carry them behind you
Like the train of a wedding dress.

ULTRAMARINOS

Now that you're conscious, naturally you're annoyed.
You feel like shit, your hair sticks to your head,
your mouth's an abbatoir. So my paseos begin
to find what might help you feel more human:
shampoo, a toothbrush, good chocolate.

Past the crowding buddleia and the teeming carpark
runs a lane. Hopeful, I walk along
and along, past the little villas, barking dogs,
electrified gates and down a hill
- why are good things often down a hill? -

to where the Ultramarinos, cave-shop, lies,
still and dark, cramful with answers to your needs,
guarded by a smiling woman behind a wooden counter
waiting for me to ask. Whatever I ask for
will be there. Even, crepuscular,
the huge church candles for fiestas
that they crown with Vittel bottles against the weather.
If they have those, then, toothbrush, shampoo, easy!

She searches at the back to find the chocolates,
in the unfathomed time-zone before supermarkets
where she reigns as a goddess of merchandise,
smiling, granting your needs now you are conscious,
in her quicksilver world between states, her ultramarinos,
her soft *no te molestes*, my *gracias*.

THE COMPOSITION OF TEARS

Tears are blue
and creamy from the glacial flour.
Sacred from the volcanic core
and filtered slowly
through the beds of peonies
that line your lungs.

Tears well up or down
depending on the depth
of your water table.
If you are Iceland
or Yellowstone Park
they spurt under pressure.
If you are a ley line
they are pools where the moon is reflected.

They transform your landscape into softness.
They are a solution to bitterness.
Liquid where bitterness transfigures itself
into something from the sea.

'I LOVE THE EARLY MORNINGS'

— wrote my friend,
of the times he rose to leave his lover
before her children rose. Here,
by the open hospital window,
you do not rise. I pour
orange juice and manzanilla tea
down your barely-woken throat.
You do not rise. I sit by you
under the cool Galician morning.

THE HOSPITAL CAFE

That's how I think of it, though I had to leave the hospital
And walk through a carpark and a little wood,
Eucalyptus and pine, strewn with empty water bottles
To find it. Past a broken place

With hides hung out to dry, and down an incline
Where begonias and marigolds grew, into a dark bar
With Spanish lace at the windows, where a quiet waiter
Laid white linen quickly. Inside

We all looked the same,
Heads down, dying for some real food,
Hardly able to ask, but asking
When the waiter asked *Que quieres?*

What we wanted
Was for the sick one to recover.
But no one could tell the future
So all we did was our time in the hospital

And, since there was nowhere for us to sleep but chairs,
Lift our spirits with *raciones* and a little wine.
Head down, dying for some real food
We walked through the little wood each day

Past a broken place
With hides hung out to dry.

MOTHER, DEAD

I found her perfected by a crystal lake,
her nagging transfigured to angelic advice,
her lumpy veins to alabaster,
her gossip to pearls of music.

One thing remained – her fishwife laugh,
Booming over the water.
Why are you laughing like that, now you are dead?
You'll know soon enough, said her laughter.

THE CORE DREAMERS

I imagine them
holding the world together
or dreaming it apart

because the plan
if there had ever been a plan
had gone haywire

and there were only their dreams
to save us.
They dream, perhaps,

of the immense danger of goodness,
of daring to imagine what it would be like
through the cosmic dust of moonlight

and without the hierarchy of near and far
to extend their dream
into any sleeper, anywhere.

Into the warm bend of a beloved body
(in the dream, all are beloved)
who begins to imagine now

the danger of goodness,
the danger we all will have to imagine
as none of us can be saved

except by our dreams, our love-drafts:
the air-content of our images.

MY SECOND RESURRECTION

It's the second year I've been to the Resurrection.
The first, I was astonished at the noise of the stone rolling away.
This year, the Roman soldiers marched up and down the slope
outside the closed tomb.

When they fell flat on their faces before the angel,
one of the chubby ones fell awkwardly
and rolled down the slope himself
revealing black pants and ample legs as his uniform rode up.

The crowd remained respectful
even though we'd waited an extra hour
for the Resurrection to begin,
because the soldiers, the three Marys and the disciples

didn't know the clocks had changed
the night before. My feet hurt,
balanced as I was on the steep slope
(the Roman had rolled to my feet).

But when it happened,
the music, the liberated dirty pigeons,
fireworks and cannonballs, then again,
like last year,

nothing mattered but the rising again.
I bought embroidered handkerchiefs
from a man at a little stall,
The sun hit my neck

and I walked with everyone else back down the hill
thinking, Well, that's it for another year.
A bit of a shambles,
a complete pig's ear in fact

but at least he's risen.

WHAT SHALL WE DO WITH ALL THIS WATER?

I'm dreaming of a pipeline to the desert sky,
where the maker of oases can translate this flood

into a thousand fountains, fructify
the famine with enough of everything that's good,

sprinkling the dust with plenty,
with iridescent moisture, sparkling food,

to make a dying valley
sing again. Surely the proud

rainmaker will take this superfluity
to where it's needed.

          Surely
there are roses in the air, waiting to bud,

to fall into an ecstasy
of growth, enormous blossoms dreaming backward

from dead ground to fecundity?
As the rood-

screen dreamed the mystery
of incarnation and the sacrificed god

to verify
itself a real (royal) portico of wood

between those who come to pray
and the silent place they pray to. Could

there be another world than this, I wonder, one where beauty
knows that she originates in mud

and that mud's her first reality?
And kneels, therefore, in wet dirt by sodden doors and sodden food,

aware this knowledge is her only
ark of gopher wood?

THE DOVES OF FINISTERRE

All day they've been rising and falling in front of the window,
hectic flights of lilac and pearl
and hoverings,
wondering perhaps whether to perch on the sill
or slip back down to the waste ground
where the willows wait in the coastal wind,
the silent irises exhale a lemon gold
into the cold air, wet earth.

Dove-decisions. Whether to be on watch
high up here
or down there in the busy branches,
the sea of willow leaves.
Tree-heaven or sky-heaven.
Discarded breast feathers roll down the roof-tiles
rolling softness through the house,
a sudden change of heart.

Then they're up, a whole puther of them,
pushing and pulling the air with their wings.
Are they holding the air together?
Their flock-intention, flock-purpose
suggests that nothing in this afternoon
could be here if not for them,
as the sun itself perhaps could not rise
without their urgent singing in the branches before day broke.

LEARNING TO BE DEAD IN CABLE STREET

Morning: limbs working, but still half asleep.
Mauve mist on the cobbles, blackbird quiet,
the work-drawn crowds in Cable Street muffled,
hushed in our soft somnambulance. We're all
on our way somewhere, somewhere automatic,
without thought or adrenaline. We move around
our bodies like birds, easily pneumatic,
observing boundaries, off the hook of will,
walking around asleep, vaguely mindful.
Is this what it's like to be dead? Easy?
Wrapped in such a mist of haze and weather
that everything's clear? Could Alexander
leave Diogenes alone, here, now, when Cable
Street's become the fields of asphodel?

TUBES

At Embankment we squash together,
Our breath shallow,
Hardly alive at all,
And the jaunty driver tells us

That another one has jumped under a train
At Mile End. 'Jumped' sounds so energetic
That people start to laugh
At the gusto of trampolining up to the next world.

I think of the two who made the jump
And didn't die. One slipped between the outer rail
And the electric middle rail, and fainted.
Hauled up on the platform, asked her name,

She answered, and her saviour said
'What a lovely name!' The other, more damaged,
continued with one dead arm, or one dead side,
half of him alive and half dead,
but still alive enough to father a child.

Everybody in the carriage is wobbling.
There's a throbbing, a boumboumboum,
As if we're all going to rise again.
Fuzz. Haze. Perhaps I'm passing out.

Then, relief! The man opposite's T-shirt comes into focus.
It reads 'I am a cunt. You are what you eat.'
He's slim. Obviously a healthy, but not big eater.
Something more than a big eater.

I lean back, deep in my fallopian stillness.
Shadwell, my stop, and I am still alive.

THE VISION OF ST EUSTACE

Imagine me shimmering in egg-white on wood
on my horse, blessing all the animals of my Lord.
His hound is chasing a hare
who will always escape. His other hound
turns to question me. He asks
'Should I chase this lordly stag who looks at me,
who has our Lord growing out of his head like antlers,
whose antlers seem to support His cross,
an antlerish backdrop for His passion?'

I tell him that the painter does not grasp perspective in the contemporary way
and that he should treat the stag as belonging to a receding plane
that he, golden though he is with glowing tempera, will never enter.

There is a scroll below me
to tell you, looking at all this coloured albumen painted on a felled tree,
that this is only art. The killing has already happened
or is about to happen. But it is not happening now,
where I sit on my horse with my Lord and all his animals.

GALICIAN EGGS

Galician eggs live with their mother
whom they believe to be a virgin
until they are thirty years old.
Then they are sold for thirty pesetas
and begin to perform miracles.
They make shushing sounds as I crack them – Muxia, Caixa.
They drop in the bowl
and the kitchen floods with gold.

Golden walls, golden floor, golden light
reaching for my eyes, reaching down the optic nerve,
drenching my pineal gland in gold.

It was out of a Galician egg that the world hatched.
When the world is sick, Galician eggs will save it.
They are the eggs of nature, the carbuncle of the sun,
the most noble purified earth.

THE ROSE TAKES OVER

After the fights, the lack of sleep,
the long illness that brings you close to death,
the rose, as usual, takes over.

The god of silence is silenced by the bribe of a rose
and you are free, here, in the spacious empty heart
that opens for you as it has opened for all others

who long with the longing of a lover,
not for love but for the generous open vacancy
that lies in the heart of love.

You are the wife who has lost her husband,
the wife who does not mourn, but knows,
here among his poems and his deep thrown bowls

that you both always lived somewhere else,
really, and he has left you for that place.
His departure allows you to go there sometimes

in your earthly life, as now, you rinse dishes
by the kitchen window, gazing at a rose outside
that is always blown and always coming.

THE REJECTED ADDRESSES

No one ever came to the house
and so it gradually perfected its emptiness –

invisible food nourishing the blood
of those who no longer needed to eat,

plants, their emerald chlorophyll so potent
they could realign a mind disastrously awry,

an air unbreathed except by plants,
pulsing, rich with all the requirements of human lungs.

Because the house was vacant it stood,
like all the rejected addresses, in back streets

with impossible rubbish bags
to offer its perfections.

The rejected addresses stand open, always, without expectations.
Everywhere they are offering themselves, gloriously empty

but furnished with everything, everything
I could ever set store by

as anywhere would be that was left to come to itself,
let be until it found out what it was and where.

ONE FLESH

"She was all woman, all women to me."
This, after we'd washed her at the hospital, and she'd pleaded
to come home, though he hadn't made a ramp
for her wheelchair yet, and she couldn't get her false teeth in
to eat, her gums jumping all over with the crab
that had settled itself all over.

"I'm going to die tonight," she'd said, as he held her from behind
for comfort. He held the tea-cup to her lips and countered
"Don't be daft." "I am, I am," she whispered.
He called to tell me in the morning.

I'd thought my parents' marriage
the usual pain, rocking on
through years of compromise and waste.
The flowers he brought her home from work,
his kiss as she leant against the oven
I thought an obligation.

I wasn't ready for his "She was all woman, all women to me":
my needful, salutary exclusion from their marriage.

BLOOD ORANGES

I halve and squeeze them for my breakfast,
their lovely egg and bacon red and yellow,
and see my own blood and my bone marrow
on the six glass hospital slides
like sunrises. "Oh, beautiful,"
I said to the doctor who'd taken it
so gently from my hip-bone. "Yes,"
she replied. "Even more so when it's magnified."

We sit in the bare ward, waiting,
sunrise after sunrise waiting in my bones.

FINISTERRE

As we are at the end of the world
everything here is gauged in microseconds,
the split life or death chances of Formula One.
Even the rainbows behave differently

as they would in a place where nobody came by accident.
Like Reepacheep, we are all here because we chose to be,
so the waves of light drenched in particles of water
don't recede, endlessly, as they do in the books,

but begin and end their polychrome arts
here on the rocks. Look, you can touch the source of colour,
the moment-place where sunlight offers flowers to her handmaidens
then throws them into the air on a furled carpet of purple

while underneath, a fisherman rows out in a velvet boat,
no surface tension between himself and the water.
Here, there is nothing else but this: nothing to pull us
forward, nothing back. The fishermen's knots

that held the nets in place have worked loose
and we are floating in a sea that was always waiting to receive us,
the fathomless ocean that holds neither fathers nor remorse,
here at the last landfall, where rainbows behave differently.

SAND

Sand is the final visitation
washed down from a galaxy of hills.

Diamonds, mica, verdigris of a tin can
oxidised by the rain of love, bathed by minute spills

of amber for its pale yellow, the crucifixion
of a million trees, a million mother of pearls

for their silver and grey. All the civilisation
that ever was, here between the whorls

on your fingers. All emeralds of thought, priceless stone
of innovation, all the complex ravels

of the past, slipping in their easy dispensation
between your toes, their silent stories sifting softly round your ankles.

THE WORLD IS A CHILD

The world is a child, her own child.
She realises, as she passes the scummy graffiti on the tight-packed block of flats,
The kids with their bikes and mobile phones, dealing crack,
That they are all hers. She has imagined them,

As she also imagined the dense bluish red of the tulip bursting in her bowl,
The implacable spidery bud of wisteria crawling on its giant arm up the post.

What has she not imagined?

The world is a child she beats in her anger close to death,
A child who runs to her then, covered in blood, for comfort.

For it is she who must comfort the world after the near-annihilation.

She sighs. She breathes. She wishes - wishes are hers too -
She'd known this before. It would have saved all the punishment
Of herself and everyone she loves. But she knows it now,
As she knows now what it means to know such things.

The world is a child, her own child. She says it to herself.

She sings it.

NIGHT WORK

Upstairs on the bus I hear the boy's lonely protest behind me –
'I'm not being silly Dad. I did work there,' and look up to see
the glassy mirror windows
of the vast Prudential Building where he used to work.

My daughter travelled to her work on a 73
with two invisible friends, Banbury and Thompson,
and some mornings I wake, aware
I've been at work all night, with the ache

of learning something I have to learn alone, asleep
in the dark. As when my lover's dead wife
sat with me in a dream, naked,
neither ugly nor beautiful, teaching me

what happens when we die. 'The problem is'
she told me, 'you remain in the state you achieved
when you were alive.'
In my dream I am wide awake.

I sense the angel guiding Saint Matthew's hand
while, old, arthritic, blind, half-literate,
he labours over the good news he must write
before he dies. He has no choice. He must do this

if he's to feel the joy that comes from ardour,
the life that's really worth the candle,
as Christine taught me, naked in the night.
Below, rainwater ripples on the roof of the bus shelter

and late gold leaves settle on the moving water.
A glamorous advert face reflects itself in the glass
and fondly, for a second, I think the face my own.

BREAKFAST

In the sun-filled, dust-gold room
the man and the woman sit with mugs of tea.
He reads, she looks out the window

on to the balcony where two snowdrops
hang in the hanging basket
wrapped in a web of grey-green ivy,

and a white camellia waits with its one white bud
for the time and strength to open.
The man and the woman are leaving their bodies.

The butterfly that each calls the self
has flown, yet again, somewhere else,
his to the girl being tried for killing a baby,

hers to the new shoot on the camellia
and the bud that sits like a fat white larval blob
on the bendy stem. She sits inside the bud,

inside its cold whiteness, as it waits to flower,
he inside Louise, the girl accused
as she waits to know if she is named a murderer.

They look at each other. They know
that they are elsewhere, finding out a place
they had not thought to enter, that this is what they do,

it comes with the territory of being human,
this act of leaving, of becoming someone else,
or longing, at least, to make an entry.

As they did last night, when they entered each other
in the mother of all confusion we call love.
Which is what made this breakfast possible,

these mugs of tea, this ordinary light,
this journeying into unfamiliar countries
where they neither know nor fear the lie of the land.

LEARNING TO BE DEAD

When my dead sister took my hand in a dream and invited me with
her into the land of the dead, it seemed natural to go along with her.
At first I saw nothing. There was nothing and nobody to see. But
soon, out of desire, shapes began to appear. This is what everyone
wants to know, isn't it? What it's like on the other side. Because we
could go there at any time. One slip of our foot, one faulty move-
ment in the valves of our heart, and we are there, where my sister
found herself to be when the Jaguar hit the Beach Buggy she was rid-
ing in. One moment she was a fifteen year old taking a lift home
from a party, and the next she was – not, simply not: clothed in the
extreme glamour of not being there.

All I could feel at first was the pressure of her hand. Then this was
accompanied, or replaced, by the pressure of desire. I realised that
things come to life, even in the land of the dead (then I thought,
especially there) through desire, which is the courtesy that thought
pays to feeling. A feeling arises in the heart (there, the subtle heart,
still capable, more capable perhaps, of feeling) which thought then
clothes in an image, or in images.

All through this time, she was laughing.

The problem is, we bring so little back from a dream. It's all Khubla
Khan. All I can be sure of is that, while I was there, I conversed with
my own feelings, thanks to the service of my thoughts, which made
them real to me. My feelings, sensations, pains, fears, came to me as
characters, real people I could talk to and come to know. The longer
I was with them, the more I loved them, Rachel's laughing presence
encouraging me on.

Were these dream people any less real than those I knew in my waking life? I don't think so. It's just that in death (or in this place where
I was learning to be dead) the dream people did not, in their turn,
press their own feelings back upon me, as they did when I was
awake. So, for the first time, I could own my own feelings, because I
knew that I myself had created them.

Then

Then it occurred to me that dying might involve a learning to be real, something we often don't have time to do in life, because we are so busy being confused between our own feelings and those of the person, or people, we are with. And in learning to be real when we are dead, we could also, perhaps for the first time, learn to experience love without the terror of losing who we imagine we are.

All this when we have, or so it seems, stopped being anyone.

THE SOLEMNITY OF GERMS

I am sick of my blood.
It is so thin, a wimpish pink membrane
holding me here: the net curtain at my window
flinching, teasing.
Make your mind up I say to my blood.
It is like one of the foolish virgins,
its wick untrimmed, with not enough oil.

Why do I hate my blood? Because I'm tired
of burning up inside, the fire always stoked
the lights never out. I saw a leaf today
a plane leaf. I decided to leave my shimmering country house
– let it burn down for the insurance –
and enter the cells of the plane leaf.
I've had enough of red.
I want to fall into green,
the xylum and phloem of unravelling ferns,
the still order of standing green water,
rank, teeming, full of the solemnity of germs.

AN EXPERIENCE IN STONE

After living the normal life
of hot blood, visibility, the ecstatic transformations
into nakedness, the delicate invalid camellia
inside themselves always needing water or attention
they begin their experience in stone:

molecules moving slowly and more regularly,
bumping into each other with the regularity
of carbon: memories inside each molecule
of the times they moved randomly, dancing,
hardly touching another, as the gas in the solar areola,
or when they were the sun itself
with no solid centre, only burning:

after these memories, they experience
being Chesil Beach, their hearts composed
of many stones, each unique, none cold,
with the moving temperature of weather, its integrity,
beginning themselves wherever they are found,
wherever the sea washes them or
whichever traveller takes them for his table.

YOU LET IT GO

The valley of the shadow is a place of help and no help.
There are no stimulants. You've given up your heroin
along with your morning tea. Pornography is long gone
as are the wonderful surges of envy and the adrenaline
of addictive love. Only true love remains, heavy oxygen molecules
breathing through you in a long chlorophyll river.
Much of your life is irrelevant, and you let it go.
Really there never was any other life but this one
where you are hand in hand with the bridegroom
who has come to tell you that he cannot come yet
but he will come again, and you are to stay
alone in the valley as you are: without stimulants,
with only the river to tell you there are no wants,
you lack nothing, and your cup was always
there, with water to the brim.

LATE NIGHTS IN ITHACA

Troy was childsplay compared to this cold, clear, hard place
and so were Calypso and the Pig Woman.
Being a pig isn't so bad, and charms, well,
enslaved to a nymphet has its moments.

But you get through them, don't you,
like a real bloke, and battle your way back
to the woman waiting. You sharpen your son
into a man and boot out the suitors. That's what men do.

But this. This woman looking at you. She looks.
She seems to want something so badly
you could tie yourself to the mast again.
And look at this place anyhow. It's a mess,

you don't know the rules anymore
and cleaning it up would be harder than war.
Domestic bliss.
Your eyes panic round the room

and see the table spreading out. Your table,
the same hardwood as your bed,
which can't be moved.
She's seen it too, and idly clears the flagons

to make a space.
Well, it's worth a try. It'd be a start,
until you find out
what's really going on.

And when you've finished your first voyage with her
you look down on the grain.
Beneath your knees, in appalling cacography,
you read Odysseus = Penelope O.K? and think

OK, I'll stay another night.
And she's making plans in her head
for your welcome feast, with turtles and peacocks (yawn)
which you'll elude. Never give a woman

an even break, and feasts are full of poisoners.
But you might be back, another awkward customer,
when she's not expecting you, mind,
for another trip on your wine-dark table.
She needs a lot more of everything
and she's not gonna geddit. No fear.
That's what real men do. You can look it up.

MY MOTHER NEVER WENT TO VENICE

but here, on the Rialto, I find
her cut glass beads, her crystal animals.

All the gewgaws that looked ridiculous
on our fake marble council fireplace

are fabulous in their home
of feathered masks, red velvet gondoliers

the swan dives of Venezia's football team.
Now my mother is gone

may her heaven be Venice.

May she be floating now
in a floating feathered mask

nodding to the dreaming, drumming, whistling Ultras,
the swan dives of Venezia's football players.

IN YOUR DREAM

In your dream you are everyone.
You are the woman who, inexplicably, owns a sheep
Whom she's taking for a walk. You are also the sheep.

You are the wild animals of uncertain species and ferocious habits
Whom you observe rooting at the grass verges.
You are the grass verges.

And, when the sheep, running by your legs,
Becomes your child who needs to stop, by your legs,
So that it can shit in its own woolly nappy,
You are your own child, as you are its mother,
Berating yourself for forgetting to bring the spare nappy.

Once you've made the breakthrough, you know, awake,
That you are everyone in the room.
You are the man who forgets to wash, who smells of his own piss,
The man you will ask to take a shower.
You are the woman who cannot speak for fatigue,
The man you lost, who drowned himself. All yours.

As is all the future, all the past. So when
Jesus asks his father why he has forsaken him,
You know that he has, only, for a moment,
Forgotten who he is. That he is God,
As he is the centurion, his own mother,
Judas, Pontius Pilate, who washes his hands,
And the man who forgets to wash
Whom you've just asked to take a shower.

As is your own threadbare garden
The first garden
At the beginning of the world
As you are the beginning,
As you are the world.
Now, on this February afternoon.
All of you.

THE MEETING

She had expectations she could never make clear
Thinking that others must know what she wants
As if they were gods and could see into her heart.

She expects them to act upon her, rather than her act,
Expecting miracles, the world organized around her joy.
Then, sometimes – it seems absurd – this could be right:

The longing she has for a particular face, a voice on the telephone –
And it's the one she wanted. As if the soundwaves,
The light itself had carried her, and the want was filled without asking.
She hates to ask. It feels like a defeat.

Did she ask him to come?
I think not. He just came.
But she had to allow it. She didn't ask,
She allowed him to come. His mouth a volcano
Telling of milk – his, her own. Telling her
To leave her fallow gods, her televisions,
To make her way through low, drowned land
Through the stolen places, the thieveswood

And face him by the ocean. To put on
Her own oyster death. To make a life.
Her own. An other.

BUDDLEIA ON WASTEGROUND

The church burned, the altar fell with its Christ,
And now I see the buddleia sliving out,
My feral flowers, gloved with grey from exhausts.
Their heads hang limp, their leaves arch back with thirst,
Loose-veined, ironic green hills in this drought.
I have a feathered feeling when I tread
Among them, of angels in the laddered air
That come as butterflies loitering
Round my buddliea's soiled purple. I bow
Close as monarchs to their clutch of colour,
Mauve cups lit by drops of rust. A crouched
Idea of fire lighting the rood screen
That swirls around my shoulders. In each calyx
A steeple burns and burns and does not fall.

NOTES FROM A LOST WORLD

In the dark times
Will there also be singing?
Yes, there will be singing
About the dark times.

Brecht, *Collected Poems Volume 3*

Their songs were always simple,
Alleluja and *oh*,
And some, their best, had no words at all,
But even these didn't save them
Though they sang them till the end.

When I reached the devastation trail
I saw lava from the central fountain, like water,
Running downhill. This was the fire goddess
Flowing towards her lover
Who had become a fish
And did not know she had at last accepted him.

The people walked as close as her anger permitted,
Then left gifts of gin at the boundary of their pain.
Alcohol, spirit. This was the journey they longed for
But could not allow themselves.

A few tried to hold back fire with fire,
The burning of the male with the female.
But even these lost their nerve,
As if they were on a new continent,
Too spread out to know that they were making
A good start.

And all that's left us is their songs,
Which prove that they knew what to do
Even though their courage failed them.

The life not lived, but longed for.
And all we have to go on is their singing.

CHRISTMAS MORNING UNLIKE OTHERS

He is down by the leechwells. I've seen him
In the lepers' walkway in the dark,
Dancing in his graveclothes,
Dancing his T cells back above 200,
Beating the twisted fig of his thymus,
The black gold of his bone marrow.

He knows I am waiting
For his cormorant eyes, his riptide grin
That pulls me out into the deep water
Where I want to be.
                                    But for now
Be is still unborn, alive only in the rope
Of every virus, my lord of herpes, plague,
Root abscesses, and all pain:
Alive in the death that waits as a hidden bud
In my baby's thumb.

Don't come yet! I cry. I am not ready.
I have to buy the standing stones and gather beeswax.
But he is careless as Pan. The sheep will come,
He writes on some hidden fax. He has just received
A lethal dose of chemotherapy, yet all is on schedule.
CAT scans shudder, anxiety and depression scales
Have overshot themselves, night sweats are part of the picture
And my unborn lord is shining in the golden candlestick
I do not yet own.

Come, then. Let me greet you in my red dress.
But what he wants is my unwashed skin,
The inside of my mouth, sour from sleep,
My amalgam-filled teeth, my empty breasts,
My varicose vein, my spots.

What can I give him? He is holding out
His left hand – he has the karaoke machine going –
And asks me what I want to sing.

It is the allelujah of dung beetles
Alive for my lord
Deep in the sewers of spring.

MACCHU PICCHU, CITY OF BONES

At first it is a world-dump,
Mappa mundi at her feet without the missing region.
Just drawers where the poor are put away:
TV orphans, Holland Park's abysmal cherry blossom.
All she wants is the fields beneath these tall mistakes.

Then an isthmus appears. He is kissing her
By the statue of Hermes in the British Museum,
She is driving him down some impossible road
In Chingford. The Magellan Straits are opening up,
Patagonians are here, their sandals fresh from marching

And at her feet laps El Mar Pacifico without conquistadors.
But only for a moment.

Soon the Aztecs are ripping out her heart
And he watches while she slowly ceases to beat.
She moves her small possessions into the street of the dead
And becomes a humming bird, alive on small nectar.
Not gone, but very small, small as mustard seed.

Once again the city changes. Bride Lane is holy –
This was where she ate again, a little steak and kidney –
Saint Bride's is holy – 'If the hostages can be released,
Can I too?' –And Saint Paul's – and the Market Estate,
And all that she can see from the lemon winter jasmine of her balcony.

It is Macchu Picchu, city of bones,
Winking at her through the drizzle.
Her Hegelian city, waiting to be turned to dust,
For the continents to shift, for the final architectonic stone
To move, so she can kneel again, in the garden
To a man who seems to be the gardener.

STOPPING BY WOODS ON A SNOWY EVENING IN MY MIND

Although I didn't know these woods as well as you
I knew them for a while. They were lovely, it's true,
But I didn't love them. Why, I didn't know, then.

As the cattle and sheep farmers had moved west
To Oregon, perhaps, or California, the trees were more plentiful
Than when you stopped your little horse. More trees than people,

They said. But it was scrabbly second growth,
The tamarack and cherry that run wild, that the locals
Tear up as weeds. Often, I would stand in the woods

Looking at an old cellar-hole alive with goldenrod
Or at the fireflies sparkling by the tiger lilies
And think, Why can I not love it here?

You were buried half a mile away
And pilgrims came to the New England town
To see your grave. I watched the beaver

Build her lodge across the frozen creek.
She pushed bits of ice out of the way, patiently,
And ferried twigs and sticks in her mouth

To make a brave and lovely mound
Out on her little island. That was when
I thought that I was wrong, and that I should,

Or even could, learn to love these woods. But then
A man from Fish and Game came to lay a trap,
And when I asked him why he had to kill the beaver,

He said, Pest animal. Like the Indians.
The woods then looked so clean, in my mind,
Like the disinfected locked ward of a mental hospital

That already I was packing a few things, to return
To my city, with its feral cats and city foxes,
It dirty streets and its blest confusion

At what is, and what is not, pollution.

PALINODE

'Because women in the upper storeys demand a face at the pane'
'High Talk', W.B. Yeats

I always thought, There never will be a face at the pane.
I'll sit here in this high bare room, and whatever happens
Will not be what I wanted to happen. It will be some dispiriting
Soap opera, the minutiae of human relations examined at length
With no denouement. There'll be no outdoors, no blackbirds shaking the air
At 3 a.m. Just bickering, a low-grade tragedy, and whatever perfection there is
I'll have to imagine.

What did I know?
One day I came down and a blackbird scudded across a neighbour's garden
Into winter jasmine. Witch hazel furred its feathered pods into the air,
A hellebore hid its face against a thick-bending wall of camellias
And the world was on stilts. And I came to see
That this wasn't merely the spring. It was always like this.
Always a face at the pane, if only I would come down from that room,
And whatever perfection existed was always more, always more
Than I could ever imagine.

MIRIAM'S FEVER

She wakes me in the night, fingers raging.
'The soles of my feet are burning,' she says
And sits on my bed and cries.
I go and wrap the ice in flannels.

She's lying down on the quilt
In her long T-shirt, eyelids quavering,
Hands alive with fever. I roll her sideways
And put the cold flannel against the back of her neck.

She sucks in air. I roll her back
So she can have the ice on her forehead.
Now her legs. I wipe the freezing flannel
Down each one, and wrap it round her ankles.

'Thank you,' she says. 'I'm shivering now.'
The balcony is open so the summer wind
Can cool her while she sleeps
And we spend the night top to toe

In the little bed. I feel her body
Ease back into itself. I am keeping watch,
Watching while her body heals her.

No lips like hers, no skin, no dribble
Like hers that runs from lips to pillow,
No feet or legs like hers.

No privilege like mine in bathing them.

CONVERSATION WITH HESTER

'I'm planning my evacuation to Mars,'
She says to me. 'If Hero and I
Can get the theory of hyperspacial travel right
Then Lily's cousin Joe can build the ship.
We'll have to take Lily as well
Because she might feel a bit left out if we took her cousin.
There was a problem over how to recruit others
Because we didn't want to say
Do you want to come to Mars
Because then they'd tell people
So I decided we'd just go
Then observe them from Mars
And when we'd decided who we wanted
Just come down and get them
Making out we were aliens.
And we wouldn't take you
Because you're a poet
And you'd use up all the oxygen
That we'd had to make out of nothing.
And if we wanted poets
We'd come down and abduct some good ones,
Except all the good ones
Are grumpy old men.'

RUBAIYAT FOR MIRIAM

I thought you would not return to me, my
Daughter, by your look, your eyes so angry
That I had left you there with your father
While I began to live without the lie.

It seemed a cauterized wound. You'd held
A candle to your broken part, to seal
Me out. You pulled yourself away, and would
Not offer me your hand. I thought you'd healed

Yourself, or pushed the wound deeper inside,
A poisoned itch your clenched young skin could hide
For years – for ever? –until that last night
When I came to your bed and asked if you'd

Let me lie with you a little while. You
Rolled your eyes to heaven, then muttered, 'Oh
All right, just half an hour.' I watched you fall
Asleep, your seven-year body letting go

Into our last night together. Then I
Slipped my arms around you, thinking *Only
This one night. I have to print your face, your body
Deep into my mind so I can never*

*Lose the sense of what it's like to have you
Here with me.* I did not sleep. There was so
Little time, Miriam. Then, towards dawn,
You turned to me and seemed to melt. I drew

You very close, you wrapped your arms around
My neck. When you opened your eyes I found
They'd overflowed in streams down your nightclothes.
At first we looked in silence, then the sound

Of your voice saying 'This is the worst day
Of my life' and 'I want to go with you.'
No tickets left. Nowhere for you to stay
If you came back with me. But then I knew

That you would return when I'd found a room
For you, a safe place for us to be in.
A flower opens inside me as I search
For a home for us. Soon, Miriam, soon.

WHAT THE NEW YEAR SANG

Don't rush me.
I am a man whose body is numb
From lack of love: mine, others'.
At first all I know is the pain of being touched
Or nothing –
I won't know you are there at all
At the places where my shell has thickened.
Come back to those places.
Under the narcosis lies something that cannot bear to be loved.
You must attend to it, no matter how it looks,
Smells, sounds or feels. Taste it.
Inside my body
                          is joy. I can't feel it myself.
You must feel it for me at first.

Making me new will take all your strength and cunning.
When you speak to me, let it not be in any language.
When you lie with me, have no side.
Be loose, loose and watchful,
Patient and eager, with your lamp ready

Because when I come nothing can ever be the same,
You alive inside me, I inside you,
My days your days,
Your blood dripping on to my earth,
Milk flooding your open mouth,
January light -

TO WHOM CAN YOU TALK RUBBISH?

If you can't talk rubbish to the hairdresser,
To whom can you talk rubbish?

This one has a copy of Graves' Greek Myths
By her mirror, but she's not happy with them.

They talk too much about the different versions of the stories
And she wants the stories themselves.

                                  In the gym,
Where she worked before, all the men were Narcissus.

Did Tiresias help Jason get the Golden Fleece?
Should she use spray-on conditioner

To help my falling hair? There's a little girl
Been stolen. The police have found her.

Demeter got her daughter back part of each year.
When do you let them out alone?

What when they want a boyfriend? Psyche worked so hard
For Eros, no wonder she fell down asleep.

It's hard work, isn't it, being with someone?
I know, why don't you have Jackie Onassis flick-ups?

In this job, your arms ache,
Especially blow-drying long thick hair.

The Gorgons, imagine doing theirs!
You'd need homeopathy to protect you from the snakebites.

Bushmaster venom, what's it called? Lachesis. Ah, yes.
The spinner of the Fates.

What are her sisters called? Clotho and Atropos.
That's me, the one with the scissors.

GETTING THE DEAD

Shall I call you, sister, mother? I know
That you are close to me. It is the day
Of the dead. I've read that there are furrows
In the universe where you might hide,
The afterglow, they say, of the first command,
Let there be light. I want you to come to me.
I am alone in this hired room.
Come, mother, with your daughter, the one we lost.
I've lit the beeswax candle, but I'm drifting,
One of those souls condemned to blow about.
Wrap your subtle bodies round me. Hold me down.
I want your weight to make me gravid, have you enter me
As I will enter you tonight. Give me a baby
From the far side, to lie beside the one I've lost.
Make me labour in the field we did not set our hands to.
Earth me. Pour your honey over me until I'm healed.

HER SECRET LIFE

As she could really neither read nor write, we were surprised when we discovered our mother's notebooks, years after she died, stacked in a corner of the outhouse. There were no words in them, just brief, unfathomable bits of alphabet which she seemed to lose patience with after a few pages. (Her schooling had been interrupted at an important point by an abscess on her thigh, and perhaps she never bothered after that.) Then followed pictograms, grim and sacred-looking, more complex and convoluted as they went along. Then she'd glued down a piece of cloth that still smelled of something, and this seemed to be the turning-point, when she abandoned symbols entirely and went for things in themselves: teeth, nail-clippings, smears of dark blood. The dates (she understood numbers) told us who they belonged to.

There was even a piece of suede from my sister's shoes, decorated in biro by moons and stars.

All the sheddings of her children's bodies, gathered against time.

What I liked most was that when we found the notebooks, we thought we'd found her secret life. We mined them for crimes and lovers, an unknown career, a taboo habit. Then in our hands they yielded easily after the first abstractions, and we found only her life with us. We were her secret life.

But there were so many notebooks, very heavy. It must take just as long to hold a life as it takes to live it. So when we cleared the house, we let them go.

Talking of it later with our father, however, we heard of other notebooks. But these he kept for himself. These, he told us, were only for a husband. We'd understand his wish for privacy when we loved someone as much as she'd loved him.

Plead as we might, he wouldn't show us. He said we'd learn nothing from them. He said the children had to learn these things for themselves. Each generation came upon the secret again, if they were lucky. But you couldn't teach it. You could only feed the ground in which the secret life could grow.

FOG

Light ripples on the ceiling
From the fountain in the round coiled bowl.
Ripple. As the light inside me opens and closes.
I stare upwards

Moonstruck, varying between open and closed,
My heart aching as it did when I was chased
Home, high on a limb with nothing but my own desire.
Outside, there's nothing past my balcony

Only opaque white light against the glass.
Where are the buildings? Where's Saint Paul's?
Nothing I know about is here.
I can use my eyes and hands

But they only tell me what's inside,
Where I am. The outside world is dense.
This fog must have come for something,
maybe to say how lost I am, really,

Maybe to wink at me and say
How about a little ignorance?
Which would be all right but for the rippling
Down all my arterial lines, the turmoil made

In my capillaries: fingers, thumbs, toes –
And my half-longing for the old clarities.
But they've gone, and though I'm lost, I'm glad.
I want new words, which may or may not come.

I can't know now. All I can see's this dense, bright air.
Nothing emerges. The rippling inside. Prayer.

IF LIONS COULD SPEAK TO US WE WOULDN'T UNDERSTAND THEIR LANGUAGE.

Attributed to Wittgenstein.

There was a pain in the room somewhere
And also a lion. We didn't know
Whether the pain was part of the lion
Or whether both were part of our own bodies.
There were others in the room,
People we'd loved and still loved
And they too seemed to be part of
His beautiful aching body
That moved and moved to ease itself
And finally came to rest, a rest of giving up,
giving in, of not being able to make another move.
It was only then that something was said
In a real language, but what it was,
Or whether it was spoken by the lion,
The pain, or we ourselves,
None of us knew. Only
That something moved inside us
And the lion moved his lovely mouth.

ANIMALS

Speak to me in a language where every word
Ends with an O and the hood goes down
On my understanding. Make me ignorant.
I don't want to know what you are saying
Only the sounds you make. And I don't want
To be human, but a cat, perhaps a cat
Who has waited for just your voice and
The language of your hands. Speak to me in
Code, as you would to a gorilla mute with grief.
As you would speak to animals,
Softly, knowing you can ease them, not with
Words but with the meaning of the music under words.
Let your tongue be foolish on me.
Let me cleave to the roof of your mouth.

VIPERS IN LOVE

It is a steep climb to the anchorite cells
Through mists of brimstone butterflies, smells
Of sage and juniper. Wild boar feed
Near the path, brown, bristly, their babies
Big as cats, and a dead viper, her underside
Bright silver, lies at my feet
Like a chaste and plaited wedding necklace

For a meeting that waits in the air. I follow you,
Afraid, more tired, into these words, that come
Like scented meat, or the reek of the birthing room
Where everything begins. You are always ahead,
A little further in the trees, testing me onwards,
Knowing I will come to you, to the cells
Where monks endured a biting cold, and under that

A mute invisible love streaming down the slopes
Of their mountain. As mine streams now,
Moving dangerously through the branches, the olive and brown
Of a viper waiting to whip me in the face.
Because I have chosen this, that gives me pain
And brings me naked to you in this bitter,
Ruined, parched, once-holy place.

A DREAM OF FAIR MEN

I am the head of a Banana Republic
But we are having a military coup.
I run to my palace. Gunshot.
The General is there in confused occupancy.
I learn that I am to be his prize.

'OK, OK, I will go to that room with you.
(He has greasy red hair. I quite like him.)
But I'll have to pick up a few things first.
Stay there.' I drift around the corridors
Chatting with my staff, who do not seem aware

That power has changed hands. When I return
He is waiting for me on a dirty pallet. Most appealing.
I lift off my nightdress and lie by him
But we have absolutely no privacy. People enter
Or leave the room, talking to us. He tells me

That he loves me and he will give me a child.
I am flattered, but my childbearing days are over.
He is unperturbed. He takes from his pocket
A substantial slab of chocolate. We eat.
Because this is only a coup, after all,

Not a revolution. A revolution is not a dinner party.

ANGEL WRESTLING

Angel threw me naked across his shoulder
And galloped round the flat in full view
Of the spilling pub across the road.
When I shut myself in the bathroom
Angel picked up the hall entryphone
And said *All right, I'll tell her. No problem,*

Then barged in and yelled *The landlord*
Thinks you should behave. Angel almost
Broke my neck between his legs, rigid
With arched-back pleasure. *If you hear a click*
Just carry me to hospital, I whispered.
It'll be quadroplegia. I will, said Angel
If they'll put us in the same bed.

Angel spat wine and water over me,
Rubbed a broken peach down my spine
Then swallowed. He kept me in his belly
Three days, three nights, then threw me up at Nineveh,
Expecting me to do the business. Which I did,
Knowing by then that angels need respect
As well as wrestling. As do whales.

THIS IS WHAT IT IS LIKE NOW

Now I no longer have the half-minute on waking when you are not here.
Sleep soaked you up, there were thirty seconds in each day
When I was alone. I felt all the liberty of not having you inside me
Just at the moment when you opened the door and came back in
Now not even that. In dreams I stretch out my arms and behind me
At my fingers' ends are your lips kissing them as they open backwards
To the light. I hold you as a baby, as a boy and as you are,
A young man under the water of his life. Only as an old man
Have I not held you, because when you are old I shall have gone
Already and so there is no place for that dream in my dream.

WOLF

Sometimes at night I think you are crouching in the pinewoods
By the swamp. Above the continuo of cicadas I hear you whistling.
You are whistling me to come to you. Through the blinking
Of fireflies I can see your light signalling me, saying you are
Nearby. I wander in the garden under the Perseiad showers
That make their way behind the clouds, and I call to you.
I don't know what to call or what to say, because I found you
In a place where there are no words. But like a wolf
I throw back my head and call. Like a wolf who has lost her mate
I call and call and wait for you to answer.

SALAMANDER

A dark angel in the old asparagus patch
Overgrown with golden rod, marjoram, wild mushrooms,
Bending his dark wings over me.
Though I am bitten by insects,
My arms infected with the blisters of poison oak,
Though my bare feet bleed from the slippery rocks,
A dark angel waits with his dark wings waiting
To cover me in the silence of his pack of coyotes,
Stabbing my night with weeping vowels
And I cannot help but go to him.

Leaving my flute, my martini,
My children, their monopoly game,
To be thrown into the air and caught in some backbreaking hold,
To be forced into the forest of my own free will,
Running until he scoops me up, until the branches hit my face,
Running until he pushes me down in the mud of the swamp
And rolls me with the frog, the beaver, the salamander.
Until the swamp bursts into flame and my hair stands up from its roots,
Solid columns of fire that only he can see. Until he has killed me
And I can be alive again.